border to border • teen to teen • border to border • teen to teen • border to border

TEENS IN SOUTH AFRICA

Teens in South Africa

by David Seidman

Content Adviser: Rachel Bray, Ph.D.,
Centre for Social Science Research,
University of Cape Town

Reading Adviser: Alexa L. Sandmann, Ed.D.,
Professor of Literacy, College and
Graduate School of Education,
Kent State University

Compass Point Books ✛ Minneapolis, Minnesota

Compass Point Books
151 Good Counsel Drive
P.O. Box 669
Mankato, MN 56002-0669

 This book was manufactured with paper containing at least 10 percent post-consumer waste.

Editor: Julie Gassman
Designer: The Design Lab
Photo Researcher: Eric Gohl
Cartographer: XNR Productions, Inc.
Library Consultant: Kathleen Baxter

Art Director: LuAnn Ascheman-Adams
Creative Director: Keith Griffin
Editorial Director: Nick Healy
Managing Editor: Catherine Neitge

Author's dedication: To those world travelers Marvin and Phyliss Seidman

Library of Congress Cataloging-in-Publication Data
Seidman, David, 1958–
  Teens in South Africa / by David Seidman.
    p. cm. — (Global connections)
  Includes index.
  ISBN 978-0-7565-3854-5 (library binding)
    1. Teenagers—South Africa—Social conditions—Juvenile literature.
    2. Teenagers—South Africa—Social life and customs—Juvenile literature.
    3. South Africa—Social conditions—21st century—Juvenile literature.
    4. South Africa—Social life and customs—21st century—Juvenile literature.
    I. Title. II. Series
    HQ799.S5S45 2009
    305.2350968—dc22   2008009480

Visit Compass Point Books on the Internet at *www.compasspointbooks.com*
or e-mail your request to *custserv@compasspointbooks.com*

Table of Contents

Pretoria

Bloemfontein

Cape Town

MOROCCO

Canary Islands

WESTERN SAHARA

MAURITANIA

SENEGAL

GUINEA

SIERRA LEONE

IVORY CO

LIBERIA

BRAZIL

ATLANTIC
OCEAN

TUNISIA
MALTA
CYPRUS
LEBANON
SYRIA
IRAQ
IRAN
ISRAEL
JORDAN
KUWAIT
OMAN
ALGERIA
LIBYA
EGYPT
U. A. E.
OMAN
NIGER
CHAD
SUDAN
BENIN
NIGERIA
CENTRAL AFRICAN REPUBLIC
OGO
CAMEROON
EQUATORIAL GUINEA
UGANDA
KE
O TOME & PRINCIPE
GABON
CONGO
DEMOCRATIC REPUBLIC
OF THE CONGO
RWANDA
BURUNDI
TANZANIA
ANGOLA
MALAWI
ZAMBIA
MOZAMBIQUE
MADAGASCAR
ZIMBABWE
BOTSWANA
SWAZILAND
LESOTHO
SOUTH AFRICA

SOUTH AFRICA IS, IN SOME WAYS, A TEENAGER. You could say that the nation was reborn in 1994, when its citizens ended a government system called apartheid. This system, in force since the 1940s, made nonwhite citizens live apart from white citizens. But it did more than that. Apartheid clamped down on nonwhites' ability to work, travel, attend school, and even marry across the so-called color-bar. Often the restrictions were enforced with brutal violence.

In 1994, Nelson Mandela, the first president of post-apartheid South Africa, declared the diverse country "a rainbow nation at peace with itself and the world." Today about one of every six people in the rainbow nation—nearly 7 million of a total population of about 44 million—is a teenager. They're the first generation in 50 years to live in freedom.

Not that their lives are easy. Millions of South African teenagers face painfully high rates of poverty, disease, and pregnancy. But they're also sports fans, music lovers, students, daughters, and sons, just like teenagers elsewhere. And as they grow up, so does their teenage country.

9

Though South Africans value education, the country's schools face many challenges, including attracting enough teachers.

1

The Struggle for School

IN NOVEMBER 2007, FLOODS DESTROYED LARGE AREAS OF SOUTH AFRICA'S SOUTHERN COAST. In places such as the waterfront resort town of Knysna, emergency crews rushed in to rescue people as rising waters washed away roads and bridges.

At the same time, police officers and volunteers braved the floods to deliver sealed packages full of test questions. In Knysna and other flood-battered towns, teenagers straggled into high schools and other buildings to take their matrics—exams that would determine whether they could qualify for college.

This is just one example of the importance of schooling to South Africans. Teenagers see school as a path to good jobs. And the government spends more on education than most other nations do—nearly 20 percent of its entire yearly budget, about 100 billion South African rand (U.S.$12.9 billion).

matrics
mah-TRICKS

History Lessons

Nelson Mandela

Today's South Africa continues to feel the effects of apartheid, a system developed by white South Africans. White people first came to South Africa in the late 1480s, when Portuguese sailor Bartholomeu Dias reached the Cape of Good Hope, the African continent's southernmost tip. Europeans didn't settle in the area until 1652. That year an expedition under Dutch merchant Jan van Riebeeck—working for an international trading house called the Dutch East India Company—founded a port near the Cape of Good Hope. Today that port is the major city of Cape Town.

The Dutch controlled the area around Cape Town until the early 1800s, when British armies and settlers began pouring in. To emphasize that they had settled the area first, the Dutch began calling themselves Afrikaners. The British, the Dutch, and other Europeans spread north, starting a long series of battles with the native Africans for control of the land. The fights intensified after 1867, when diamonds were discovered at Kimberley, almost 600 miles (965 kilometers) northeast of Cape Town.

After 1879, when the British crushed the large and fierce Zulu armies, white control over the region solidified. British and Dutch forces fought each other for mastery in the region until 1910, when the British finally won. South Africa became a mostly independent part of the British Empire. Shortly afterward, white South Africans began enacting laws restricting the freedom of black Africans. In 1948, the local government formally organized the laws into the system of apartheid. This government system remained even after South Africa became completely independent of Britain in 1961.

The natives fought apartheid. As the decades passed, they launched protests and uprisings, often inspired by political leader Nelson Mandela. Finally in 1994, South Africa ended apartheid and set up a government devoted to freedom and equality.

Yet in 2006, the Institute of Justice and Reconciliation—an organization that promotes communication among African nations—reported that nearly 80 percent of the country's elementary schools, middle schools, and high schools weren't giving their students the skills they need to function as adults. If South Africans value education, why is their education system—nearly 30,000 schools and 12 million students—in such trouble?

Under apartheid, the government offered very poor schooling for nonwhites—when it bothered to teach them at all. Since most South African students are nonwhite, apartheid left behind an education system that didn't have many qualified teachers, clean and safe buildings, or high-quality books and other equipment. Improving those conditions in thousands of schools is a long, slow process.

Years, Weeks & Days at School

South African teenagers either dread January or look forward to it. The first month of the calendar year is also when the school year begins. January is summertime in the Southern Hemisphere nations like South Africa, so the start of the school year is a frustrating time for students (or "learners," as South Africans call them). Many would rather be swimming and sunning. Instead they sit in classrooms, wearing their uniforms of white shirts, blue jackets, and blue pants or skirts.

The school year runs through November. It's a long term, but learners do get some time off, particularly for the dozen major national holidays. Before or after the biggest celebrations, most schools shut down for several days. For instance, there's an Easter break in March or April and another break around Heritage Day on September 24, plus the entire month of December for Christmas vacation. Whenever any holiday falls on a Sunday, learners get the following Monday off as well.

Elementary school, known in South Africa as primary school, includes grades 1 through 6. Many primary

Children learn together in a mixed-race primary school, something that would have been unheard of before 1994.

schools also offer a kindergarten called Grade 0 or Grade R (for "reception"). High schools, which South Africans often call secondary schools, offer grades 7 through 12. Some school systems also offer middle schools that include a grade or two from primary school and a grade or two from secondary school. The government requires learners to stay in school until they reach age 16. For most of them, that means the end of Grade 9.

Classes run from Monday through Friday. There's no single schedule for all South African schools, but most of them start their day by 8:30 A.M. The school day runs about six hours, with a short break in the morning and a longer one in the early afternoon. After school comes homework, from one to two hours per night.

Required Courses

Most teenagers take a variety of courses; often they have six or seven subjects. Quite a few of the nonwhite learners are the first people in their families to master reading and writing. South Africa has 11 official languages. Learners have to study at least one of them, usually Zulu, Afrikaans, or English. Understanding English is especially important, since it is the main language for business and government.

The schools also emphasize science, an area in which South Africa suffers a skills shortage. There are not enough people trained to work in

engineering and industries that depend on mathematics and technology. The national government wants the schools to develop a work force that can handle these subjects. Banking and finance are important to South Africa as well, and schools train learners in

School children wait to tour Constitution Court, South Africa's highest court. The entrance sign features all 11 of South Africa's official languages.

subjects such as business and accounting. Most schools don't focus much on athletics or arts during the school day. However, many campuses offer after-school programs in sports, drama, and music.

On Campus

South Africa is one of the world's 25 biggest nations, at 470,000 square miles (1.2 million square km). Consequently, there's no such thing as a typical secondary-school campus. For instance, schools in places without

Schools often must improvise to serve students. Three classes in a school in the Eastern Cape province were held in three unusable buses, with no wheels and broken windows and doors.

much money can't always afford to buy equipment or hire good teachers. Rural schools are particularly known for being underfunded, while urban schools, especially in traditionally white neighborhoods, are usually better off.

In addition, South Africa has another type of school. Under apartheid, the national government forced non-white South Africans (mostly blacks) into suburban slums called townships. These areas, often outside major cities, had few if any high-quality schools.

Some had no schools at all. Today most large townships have schools, but they provide a lower level of education than schools in white neighborhoods.

Despite these differences, most South African schools do have a few things in common. For instance,

Leaving It All Behind

Nearly half of all South African high school students drop out before graduation. Part of the problem is poverty: Some learners can't afford books, uniforms, and school fees. Another problem is teenage pregnancy. About one-third of all South African girls give birth by age 20. Faced with the burden of parenthood, many of them leave school, and very few ever return.

teachers expect their students to be respectful. Some teachers allow more participation than others, but in general the teachers speak and the learners listen.

Unfortunately, qualified teachers are in short supply. The school systems can't find and hire enough educators to replace the thousands that leave every year. Part of the problem is HIV (human immunodeficiency virus), a disease that causes the deadly condition AIDS (acquired immune deficiency syndrome). South Africa has the world's highest rate of HIV and AIDS. The largest group of South Africans suffering from these ailments is 25 to 34 years old—the age of most new teachers.

In addition, schools suffer from crime. The national government's Human Rights Commission reported in 2007 that more than 40 percent of all young South Africans had been the victims of crime in the past year, and school was the single most common place where the crimes happened. Many learners, especially in poor areas, complain of robbery and assault.

Some of the worst crimes are connected to drugs, particularly in urban areas. Addicts steal from classrooms and sell the stolen items to buy drugs. Meanwhile, dealers sell drugs on city playgrounds. "I can walk into any school—you name the school you like, primary or high—and within 15 minutes, I will have bought some drug," Quintin van Kerken, a spokesman for a drug rehabilitation clinic in Johannesburg, said in 2006.

To escape these problems, some parents send their children to private schools. South Africa has more than four times as many private schools today as it had when apartheid ended in 1994. Private schools can be expensive, though, and the vast majority of parents can't afford them.

To the Matric ... and Beyond

The last year of secondary school is Grade 12. As the school year ends in November, the weather warms up. But thousands of South African teenagers feel the shivering chill of stress as they study for the matric.

The matric is a series of exams near the end of Grade 12. The name comes from the word *matriculation*, which means enrolling in higher education. Matric exams test learners on English and other languages; sciences such as physics, chemistry, and biology; mathematics; the arts; and business-related subjects such as economics and accounting. Some exams—English, for example—are required for everyone who takes the matric, while other sub-jects are optional. Students who intend to go into the sciences, for instance, usually don't bother to take any of the arts exams.

The matric is so important that many South Africans call Grade 12 the "matric year" and refer to 12th-graders as "matrics." Anyone who wants to attend

a South African university has to do well on the tests. Even some employers who don't require a college degree want job applicants who have passed the matric. As a result, most 12th-graders—about 600,000 every year—take the tests.

Graduates attend a formal event, their matric dance, often held the last Friday evening before the matric exams are given.

When the government announces the results in late December, about one-quarter to one-third of the matric takers find that they've failed. People who do not pass the matric, or who don't bother to take it at all, have a much higher unemployment rate than those who pass. The ones who pass, though, can apply to tertiary school—colleges, universities, and other places of higher learning.

They may not stay long, though. A study by South Africa's Human Sciences

Teen Scenes

The lives of teens in South Africa are vastly varied, depending on their ethnic and financial backgounds. Consider the following scenarios:

It's a warm afternoon in the wealthy suburb of Sandton, near Johannesburg, South Africa's biggest city. White kids pour out of Redhill, a private school that teaches children from some of the country's richest families. Several of them are on their cell phones, text-messaging friends via the popular service MXit, sending pictures, or just talking. One of the girls heads for the school's parking lot. The 17-year-old 11th-grader slips into her BMW M3 and rolls toward the Sandton City mall. She spends the afternoon there with friends. When she gets home, she finds that the maid has tidied her room, just as she expected.

About 870 miles (1,400 km) southwest of Johannesburg, in the township of Khayelitsha, another teenager is also leaving school. But this teen is not sure that she'll return. As the black girl walks the miles from her run-down public school to the tin-roof shack that she calls home, she's careful as always to avoid streets known for gang members and other criminals. She steps past pushcart peddlers selling auto parts and small pieces of furniture, street vendors grilling lamb and beef, housewives chatting while washing laundry in the open air, and unemployed men hanging around bars and *shebeens* (unlicensed and illegal liquor stores). But she barely notices any of them. The teenager has recently learned that she's pregnant, and she's worried. Ever since AIDS killed her parents, she's been running her household. She's been able to stay in school only because her grandparents receive a government pension. With a new baby, she won't have the time or energy to keep taking classes.

In a rural village roughly halfway between Khayelitsha and Sandton, a black teenage boy is also walking home, but not from school. He has already dropped out to help his family make a living and avoid poverty. He lives in farm country, and he has just left the local cannery. He was hoping to find a job, but too many other job-hunters had gotten there first. Still, the teenager isn't downhearted, because he's planning an adventure. Like other country kids, he wants to move to a city and find a new life there.

shebeens
sheh-BEENS

Research Council found that only 15 percent of the country's college students complete their studies and get their degrees. South Africa's universities, which rank among the best in the world, are expensive to attend. Most students simply don't have enough money. Although the government offers some financial aid, up to 50 percent of college students drop out during their first year.

The University of Cape Town is the oldest university in South Africa.

Many South African teens grow up surrounded by the natural beauty of their country.

2 Days in the Lives

LIFE IN SOUTH AFRICA CAN BE ROUGH FOR TEENS. Crime, drug abuse, poverty, disease, and other problems attack them far too often. Still, a survey by South Africa's University of Witwatersrand has found that 95 percent of the country's teens are proud of their nation. In particular, they praised the nation's people and natural beauty.

They weren't blind to their country's problems. When the survey asked, "What would be the first thing you would do as the President of South Africa?" about half said that they would try to lower the country's high rates of unemployment or crime. At the same time, the majority expected South Africa to have a rich and shining future.

South Africa's 7 million teenagers number roughly 15 percent of the population. There's no way to sum up a group that large as if they were all alike. Still, most South African teenagers have certain things in common.

Morning, Afternoon & Night

In general, a South African teen's day begins with making breakfast, tidying up the home, or doing a little last-minute homework or studying. Then it's off to school. After school, teenagers are usually on their own because their parents are out working, looking for work, or otherwise absent. A minority of teenagers—the ones who have money—can spend the afternoon having fun with friends. Most other South African teens, however, head home to prepare dinner or take care of other chores. After dinner, there's usually an evening's worth of homework.

Not everyone in South Africa follows the same daily schedule, of course. There are a lot of ways of life in a place as big as South Africa.

Home Life

The United Nations Development Program gathers and distributes information to help governments and other organizations reduce poverty, treat illnesses, and spread democracy. The organization's Human Development Index (HDI) measures how long people in 177 countries live, how well they're educated, and how much money they make. In 2005, South Africans ranked at number 121—in the HDI's lowest third.

By most measures, though, South Africans live in the richest, most modernized nation among the nearly 50 African countries south of the Sahara Desert. In 2007, 80 percent of the

In communities where homes have no running water, residents may share a watering place.

nearly 13 million South African homes had electricity, and 89 percent had piped-in running water. On the other hand, only about 60 percent had a flush toilet. About one-quarter of the homes in the Eastern Cape province have no waste facilities at all, not even a bucket or dirt pit.

The average household is three or four people, and most of the nation's

homes are small. In fact, 15 percent aren't formal houses at all, but one-room shacks. As a result, most South African teenagers don't have much privacy from the other people in their home. A few—those who live in wealthy families—may get too much privacy from the outside world, though. Throughout South Africa, homes and other buildings have high walls, gates, or fences to keep out thieves. Teens who live behind these walls struggle with not being allowed to move around on their own.

Between the South Africans who live in dirt-floor shacks and the ones who live in high-walled houses, there's a wide and growing income gap. Although the country has a sizable middle-income class, the richest 20 percent of South Africans control more than 60 percent of the country's wealth, while the poorest 20 percent controls only 3 percent. More than half of all South Africans live in poverty. They don't earn enough to buy adequate food, clothing, and shelter. The divide between rich and poor is so wide that the United Nations and other authorities rank South Africa as the world's sixth most unequal country.

Country Life

"I spent days breathing in dry, dusty air heavily tainted by wood smoke, there was no electricity, promised hot water was never actually delivered, [and] sawdust and other stuff was continuously dropped on me by the woodborers and other insects living in the thatched roof." That's how Robin Mackey, a young Canadian ecologist, has described rural life in South Africa.

About half of all South Africans live in rural areas. During the 20th century, white authorities forced blacks into ranges called Bantustans. These areas covered large chunks of the country's eastern half. One of them, the Transkei, measured about 16,500 square miles

Luxurious houses sit on the clifftops of the city of Knysna.

In rural areas, gathering water is often part of daily chores.

(42,735 square km)—about the size of Denmark. Most people in the Bantustans were painfully poor because their farmland was not fertile and paid work was difficult to find.

Rural South Africans are not doing much better today, whether they're in the former Bantustans or other areas. Many of them don't have electricity or clean running water. Jobs are scarce and often pay such small wages that many families are below poverty level. As a result, young South Africans— particularly young men—have been deserting the fields and heading into the cities.

Cities & Townships

South Africans are pouring into cities. Take the heavily urbanized province of Gauteng. Statistics South Africa, a government agency, says that more than four of every 10 people in Gauteng—41.9 percent—came there from somewhere else.

Cape Town, nicknamed the Mother City, is a physically beautiful place. Spread below the huge Table Mountain, the city sits on a peninsula that curves out into the sea and provides the townspeople with 183 miles (294 km) of coastline. It's no surprise that the town pulls in more than 6.5 million tourists

The flat-topped Table Mountain, which frames downtown Cape Town, is a popular tourist attraction.

and other visitors every year. Cape Town is also South Africa's legislative capital, where the national parliament makes the country's laws. Unfortunately, the city's rate of crimes connected to drug abuse—for instance, addicts stealing money to buy drugs—is nearly three times the national average and is one of the highest in the world.

South Africa's second most populous town, with more than 3 million people, is Durban, also known as Ethekwini. This busy Indian Ocean port is known for industries such as transportation, communications, and manufacturing. Unlike Cape Town, Durban is not famous internationally,

but South Africans are certainly familiar with it. The city attracts crowds of South African tourists who head to the town's golden beaches.

Better known than Durban is Johannesburg. With close to 3 million people, Joburg (as most people call it) is South Africa's third-largest city. It is a busy center of commerce where business-suited stockbrokers stride past small shopkeepers selling ancient herbal medicines. In this hub of high finance and towering office buildings, many people live in the sky. Joburg stands 5,751 feet (1,753 meters) above sea level; its teenagers live higher than kids in Denver, Colorado; Nairobi,

Kenya; or other high-altitude cities.

Johannesburg's neighbor Pretoria is the country's administrative capital and home to its presidency. The president has two homes, one in Pretoria and one in Cape Town, where parliament is situated. To the south is the windy, sunny Port Elizabeth, which provides work for South Africans in heavy industries such as automaking. Fifty miles (80 km) northwest of Durban live the people of the once-sleepy but now fast-growing Pietermaritzburg.

Near many of South Africa's cities are its townships. The apartheid governments set up townships to house black men who worked in cities, farms, or mines and to keep them out of the places where white people lived. Eventually generations of families grew up in the townships, and they evolved into communities with their own businesses, neighborhoods, and culture. Unfortunately, township residents are among the poorest people in the country, and their neighborhoods are the most crime-filled in the country. Many people live in shacks made of wood and plastic sheeting, with tin roofs. There is no running water inside most homes. Trash piles up in the streets, and the roads are narrow and dangerous. Jobs are hard to find and are usually in distant places. Illness is common, with AIDS growing at high rates.

The biggest township lies south-

Johannesburg is a center for mining, including gold and diamond mines.

Khayelitsha, near Cape Town, is South Africa's fastest-growing township.

west of Johannesburg. Soweto, short for South-West Town, holds about 2 million people. A collection of more than 50 smaller townships and neighborhoods, Soweto is famous for an anti-apartheid rebellion by its teenagers in 1976. Today Soweto is fighting hard to grow out of poverty. The government is paving roads and taking other steps to improve living conditions. Developers are slowly building hotels and other large-scale businesses.

South Africa's People

The idea of race has split South Africa ever since white settlers first arrived, and especially since apartheid divided the country's residents and gave superior resources and privileges to white people. But in 2007, according to the South African polling company Markinor, more than half of all South Africans—57 percent—felt that the country's often-divided races were getting along better all the time.

The government and most other sources divide South Africans into four categories: people of black African heritage, whites, "coloreds" (people of mixed race and descendants of the Asian slaves brought to South Africa in the 17th century), and Indians.

Ethnicities in South Africa

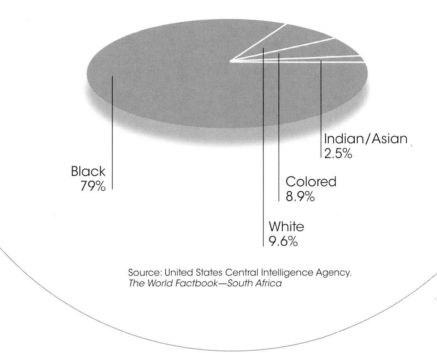

Black
79%

Colored
8.9%

White
9.6%

Indian/Asian
2.5%

Source: United States Central Intelligence Agency.
The World Factbook—South Africa

Four of five South Africans are black. They're not just the biggest racial group; they're also the fastest-growing. The fertility rate among black women is 2.92 children, while the rate for colored women is 2.27 and whites is 1.73.

Even though they're in the majority, black South Africans shoulder heavier burdens than people of other heritages. Not only did apartheid impose poverty and unemployment on black citizens for decades, but it treated them as being worth less than white, colored, and Indian people. Erasing those agonies may take a very long time. In the meantime, young black South Africans have a harder time finding a job than nonblacks. When they do find work, they generally earn less money. The national government has set up Black Economic Empowerment, a program that helps black South Africans start their own businesses and pushes companies to hire and promote black South Africans. But its progress is slow.

Ethnic Diversity

Black South Africans do not all speak the same languages or have the same origins. They fall into several tribal or ethnic groups.

Zulu—More than one-fifth of all South Africans are Zulu. The Zulu tribe has a proud and powerful heritage. In the 19th century, the Zulu ruled an African empire and defied the British armies that claimed Zulu land. Today one of the most important Zulu contributions is *ubuntu*, a unifying spirit of community and shared humanity. It is a central concept for South Africa's diverse population.

ubuntu
ooh-BOON-too

Xhosa—Most leaders of the African National Congress, the political party that has controlled South Africa's government since the end of apartheid, have been Xhosa, including Nelson Mandela. The Xhosa number more than one-sixth of South Africa's population. Their language, Xhosa or IsiXhosa, is the country's third most widely spoken tongue. (Some authorities say that ubuntu comes from Xhosa rather than Zulu.)

Pedi—Also called the Northern Sotho, the Pedi live mainly in the province of Limpopo, although some are in neighboring provinces such as Mpumalanga and Gauteng. Traditional Pedi live in tribes whose chief is the local mayor and judge. They are largely a rural people. For centuries, they lived by raising cattle. Today, however, many Pedi have found jobs far from their home ranges and villages.

Tswana & Sotho—Also called baTswana and baSotho, these two tribal groups are so closely related to each other that some authorities combine them into one group called Sotho-Tswana. The Tswana number about 3 million, mostly in North-West province and some parts of Limpopo near the country of Botswana. (Even though the country of Botswana is named after the Tswana people, South Africa has three times as many Tswana as Botswana does.) The Sotho are an even larger group, living mostly in the Free State province and in the highlands of Gauteng.

Traditional Sotho and Tswana have a strong reverence for ancestors both dead and alive. They also take pride in totems, the honored symbols of their tribes. Totems often feature a powerful animal, such as a lion or crocodile.

Other black South Africans belong to smaller groups, such as the Tsonga, Venda, Swazi, and Tswane. Each of them has its own language and culture. Tsonga families, for instance, do not expect men to do chores around the house, while Tswane people believe that men and women should share the jobs equally. If a Tsonga man falls in love with a Tswane woman, they have to work out their cultural differences or consider breaking up.

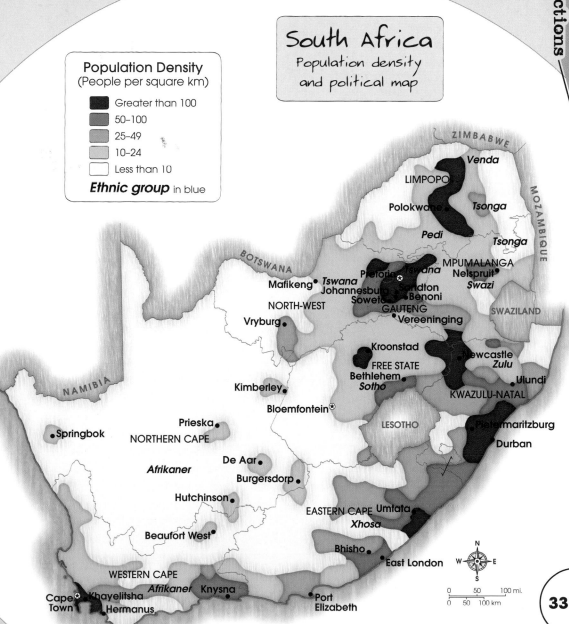

South Africa
Population density and political map

Population Density
(People per square km)

- Greater than 100
- 50–100
- 25–49
- 10–24
- Less than 10

Ethnic group in blue

ZIMBABWE

Venda

LIMPOPO

Polokwane•

Tsonga

MOZAMBIQUE

Pedi

Tsonga

MPUMALANGA
Nelspruit•

Pretoria• •*Tswana*

Mafikeng• *Tswana*

Swazi

Johannesburg• •Sandton

Soweto• •Benoni

NORTH-WEST

GAUTENG

•Vereeninging

SWAZILAND

Vryburg•

Kroonstad•

•Newcastle

Zulu

FREE STATE

Bethlehem• •Ulundi

Sotho

Kimberley•

KWAZULU-NATAL

Bloemfontein✪

LESOTHO

•Pietermaritzburg

Prieska•

•Durban

•Springbok

NORTHERN CAPE

De Aar•

Afrikaner

Burgersdorp•

Hutchinson•

EASTERN CAPE Umtata

Xhosa

Beaufort West•

Bhisho•

•East London

N
W   E
S

WESTERN CAPE

Afrikaner Knysna•

Cape✪•Khayelitsha
Town   •Hermanus

Port
Elizabeth•

BOTSWANA

NAMIBIA

| 0 | 50 | 100 mi. |
| 0 | 50 | 100 km |

33

In the Northern Cape province, teens socialize in Ornia, a private town that only accepts white residents. The villagers do not support South Africa's black government.

About 9.6 percent of South Africans are white. Most of them come from European ancestry. Dutch influence can be seen throughout the country in names such as Johannesburg. What's more, Afrikaans, the Afrikaner language, is the country's second most common language. English, the language of British South Africans, is only the fifth most popular as a spoken tongue, but it's very important on paper. It's the main language of most government documents.

White South Africans are generally better off than other groups. During apartheid, whites owned virtually all of the country's wealth and property. After apartheid, black South Africans took over the government, but much of the wealth stayed in white hands. White South Africans have some of the country's lowest rates of unemployment, teen pregnancy, AIDS, and high school dropouts.

Nearly as numerous as white South Africans are mixed-race citizens, known as colored (or "coloured," in the British spelling that South African English uses). About 9 percent of the population, colored South Africans are nearly as disadvantaged as black citizens. In some ways, they may have even bigger troubles. Studies show that colored teenagers are more likely than other South African teens to abuse the addictive drug crystal methamphetamine.

Indians form the fourth major group of South Africans. At fewer than 2 million people, they're less than 3 percent of the population, but they've made themselves known. They have some of the country's lowest rates of alcoholism, teen pregnancy, and high school dropouts.

Speaking the Languages

Batho bohle ba tswetswe ba lokolohile mme ba lekana ka botho le ditokelo.

Alle menslike wesens word vry, met gelyke waardigheid en regte, gebore.

Bonke abantu bazalwa bekhululekile belingana ngesithunzi nangamalungelo.

Each of these lines is the first sentence of the Universal Declaration of Human Rights: "All human beings are born free and equal in dignity and rights." The first sentence says it in Sotho, the second in Afrikaans, and the third in Zulu—three of South Africa's 11 official languages. Most South Africans, including teenagers, can understand at least two of them.

Here's how the 11 languages say the country's full, official name, according to the Web site GeoNative:

Afrikaans: Republiek van Suid-Afrika

English: Republic of South Africa

Ndebele (also called IsiNdebele): Repabliki we Sewula Afrika

Pedi (SePedi): Repabliki ya Afrika-Borwa

Sotho (SeSotho): Repabliki ya Afrika-Borwa

Swati (SiSwati): Riphabliki yase Ningizumu Afrika

Tsonga (XiTsonga): Riphabiliki ya Afrika-Dzonga

Tswana (SeTswana): Repabliki ya Afrika-Borwa

Venda (TshiVenda): Riphabuliki ya Afrika Tshipembe

Xhosa (IsiXhosa): iRiphabliki ya Mzantsi Afrika

Zulu (IsiZulu): Riphabliki yase Ningizumu Afrika

A Tasty Nation

Food! Teenagers everywhere love it, and South African teenagers have it in wild variety.

South Africans love meat, particularly beef and lamb, but also chicken and pork. Biltong, a popular dish, is strips of jerkylike dried meat spiced with salt, pepper, sugar, coriander, and other seasonings. *Boerewors*, an Afrikaner creation, is a fatty sausage of beef, pork, and sometimes lamb, flavored with seasonings such as nutmeg, pepper, vinegar, and salt.

Other popular dishes are *droewors* (dried boerewors, popular for snacks) and *bobotie*, a beef pie or casserole made with lemon, onion, eggs, milk, and usually ingredients such as curry powder, almonds, salt, and raisins.

Virtually every type of meat gets cooked on a *braai*, or grill. Braaiing is a national pastime, so popular that some South African corporations have started a movement to rename the national holiday of Heritage Day as Braai Day. South Africans also love turning meats and vegetables into stews and other dishes called *potjiekos*—literally "pot food," because it cooks in a metal pot.

The South African diet isn't all meat and grilling. Fruits and vegetables are popular, particularly corn. A favorite dish throughout South Africa is *pap*,

boerewors
BOOR-uh-vors
droewors
DROO-uh-vors
bobotie
buh-BOH-tee
braai
bry

Pork, lamb chops, and boerewors are cooked on a braai.

year 1500 were expert fishermen. Along with other sailors, they helped to make shellfish and other seafood important to the South African diet.

In the 1650s, the Dutch started bringing Malaysians and Indonesians to the Western Cape as slaves. The slaves added strong spices to the sometimes bland Dutch meals. In the 1800s, British settlers brought (among other things) meat pies, which are still popular. The British also took people from India to South Africa. Like the Malays and Indonesians, the Indians came with new spices, particularly the hot and popular curries.

For a final treat, there's dessert. *Koeksisters* are South Africa's version of doughnuts or churros: fried dough covered in syrup and twisted into a braid. In the big cities, South African teenagers like ice cream with chocolate sauce.

a traditional porridge from the Xhosa tribe, made from cornmeal and usually served with beans, spinach, or a tomato and onion mixture.

In addition to the Xhosa's pap and Afrikaners' boerewors, every culture that has developed in the country has given something to South African food. Millions of black South Africans enjoy samp (dried and broken corn kernels) and beans. The Portuguese explorers who came to the area around the

potjiekos
POY-kee-kos
pap
pup
koeksisters
COOK-sis-ters

37

Teen Alcohol Use in South Africa

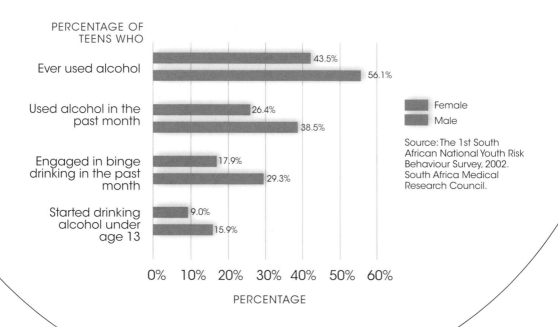

PERCENTAGE OF TEENS WHO

Ever used alcohol
- 43.5%
- 56.1%

Used alcohol in the past month
- 26.4%
- 38.5%

Engaged in binge drinking in the past month
- 17.9%
- 29.3%

Started drinking alcohol under age 13
- 9.0%
- 15.9%

0% 10% 20% 30% 40% 50% 60%

PERCENTAGE

Female
Male

Source: The 1st South African National Youth Risk Behaviour Survey, 2002. South Africa Medical Research Council.

Crime & Drugs

Although South Africans come in a variety of cultures and languages, they're almost all likely to encounter crime. South Africa's Center for Justice and Crime Prevention says that one in every seven teenagers and college students has suffered an assault such as mugging or rape. The most common crime is residential burglary, occurring 249,665 times from April 2006 through March 2007.

Some criminals steal because they cannot get work and are desperate to feed their families. Others commit their acts because of drugs and alcohol. People who are drunk or stoned often lose the common sense and self-restraint that hold people back from dangerous behavior. In addition, many addicts steal to pay for their drugs.

Most South African teenagers may not get high, but they know teens who do. Up to one-third of all South African teenagers regularly abuse drugs, according to South Africa's National Council on Alcoholism and Drug Abuse.

Alcohol is considered to be the most commonly abused drug. South Africa's legal drinking age is 18, but many teenagers start younger. A national survey released in 2004 said that 49 percent of all South African teenagers drink. (Among white teens, the rate stood at 86 percent.) A total of 23 percent—nearly one out of every four teenagers—had drunk heavily in the previous month, a percentage higher than the combined rates of China, India, Syria, Nigeria, Mexico, and the United States.

Up to one-third of all South African teenagers smoke marijuana, which South Africans call *dagga*. Other drugs aren't quite as popular, but they also affect South African teenagers. Recent years have seen an alarming growth in crystal methamphetamine, which South Africans call *tik* for the little pop that it makes when smoked. Tik stimulates its users into hours of high-energy excitement but throws them into mood swings and erratic behavior, rots their skin and mouth, and causes brain damage. It's abuse has become an epidemic in the Western Cape province, particularly among colored teens in the Cape Town area, but it has spread to other regions as well.

dagga
DAH-ka

tik
tihck

The Worst Disease

In addition to drugs and alcohol, South African teens must face the harsh reality of the disease AIDS. HIV and AIDS are so common in South Africa that "when you practice soccer with a small group of South African teenagers, at least one of them is likely to be infected with HIV/AIDS," according to journalist Laura Sessions Stepp. (Some experts say that the disease hits some neighborhoods harder than others.) Ten to 15 percent of all South Africans already have the disease; only five or six other nations have a higher rate.

The South African anti-AIDS organization LoveLife says that one of every four South African teenagers will get HIV by age 25. An additional one-quarter of them will catch it after 25. In other words, half of the country's teens today will very likely die young, their bodies wasting away in agonizing pain. Those who escape the disease may still face its effects. Many young South Africans are left alone when their parents are killed by the disease.

HIV is a retrovirus—a disease that inserts itself into healthy cells and multiplies inside them. The main medicines to slow the progress of AIDS are drugs called antiretrovirals. Unfortunately, South Africans have been slow to get these drugs. Not only are they expensive, but President Thabo Mbeki has said he doubted that HIV is the only cause of AIDS and that antiretrovirals can treat the disease effectively.

Recently, though, the South African national government published a plan to give people with HIV antiretroviral treatments by 2011. One medical journal said in March 2008 that antiretroviral treatments could save more than a million lives. South Africa may suffer horribly from AIDS now, but there is hope for the future.

Busy Bodies

South Africa's other big teen health concern is pregnancy. One of every eight teen girls is a mother. By age 20, about one out of every three South African girls becomes pregnant. Only one-third of these mothers-to-be actually want to get pregnant. For the others, having a child leads to worry

LoveLife, which provides counseling to South African teens, is a national program aimed at preventing HIV.

A 15-year-old mother faces multiple challenges; she and her baby are infected with HIV.

and fear. Many young mothers can't concentrate on schoolwork and end up dropping out. Without an education, they usually can't get a job that pays decently, and they fall into poverty and frustration.

Worries about pregnancy, AIDS, drug abuse, crime, and other problems—from the ache of poverty to the pressure of preparing for the matric exam—have pushed thousands of South African teenagers into depression. The problem strikes so deep that suicide is the second most common cause of death (after car accidents) among teenage South Africans.

Good Times

For all of their problems, most South African teenagers have a better life than their parents did. Apartheid is gone. Crime rates, while very high, have been gradually but steadily dropping since 2002. Poverty is a huge problem, but the economy is growing by about 4 percent to 5 percent per year, which means that more money is available. The University of Witwatersrand survey of teenagers found that 89 percent were optimistic about their country's future. After all, they're the ones who will create it.

After Olga Thimbela's sister and aunt died of AIDS, Olga and her husband, Pontsho Monamodi, took in their six children to raise along with their own two. As AIDS takes more parents' lives, combined families are growing more common.

3

The Closest Ties

MXIT IS BIG. PRONOUNCED "MIX-IT," it is a cheap, fast, and fun instant-messaging system for cell phones and computers. It's especially popular among the millions of South African teenagers who use it every day.

Until MXit came along in 2005, most South Africans who sent text messages from cell phone to cell phone used a service called SMS (Short Messaging Service). SMS messages could run no more than 160 characters—about the length of this paragraph's first two sentences. These messages traveled on cell phone bandwidth, like a voice conversation.

MXit sends messages via a cheaper method, the wireless Internet. It can send messages of up to 1,000 characters. The messages can reach places SMS can't, including Internet chat rooms and other online social sites. MXit carries more than 200 million messages a day from over 5 million registered users, primarily people ages 15 through 23.

MXit is just one way in which South Africa's teenagers stay close to each other, to their families, and to other people who matter to them.

Most South African teens live in a web of relationships—even if sometimes it's not easy to keep the relationships healthy.

Family Life

Compared with families in other African nations, families in South Africa are small. The average family in neighboring Mozambique has more than five children, and a typical family in Mali and Niger has more than seven. The average South African family has two or three—about the same size as families in the United States, Argentina, and Indonesia.

Africans have usually lived in extended families, where grandparents, uncles, aunts, cousins, and other relatives are a constant part of teenage lives. The British and Dutch, though, tend to

Different Cultures, Different Names

There's no official list of the most common South African first names. They come in a wide variety because of all the different languages and peoples.

Xhosa parents, for instance, have often given their children names that are Xhosa words, such the boy's name Sipho ("gift") or the girl's name Lindiwe ("have waited," as in "We have waited for her"). White South Africans of British ancestry often give their children names that are common in the United Kingdom, such as Mary and Andrew. Dumisani, which means "give praise," is a common name among Zulu boys. Other popular names are Siyabonga (for boys, meaning "we give thanks") and Ayanda (a girl's name meaning "they are many" or "they are growing").

Daankjie Jagman regularly walks his son Davan to school. Support from parents leads to greater success in school and other areas.

live in nuclear families, where parents and children live apart from other relatives. In recent decades, South Africans of all races have been leaning toward the nuclear-family model.

South African families are generally warm and friendly. South African parents, particularly fathers, have traditionally been strong sources of authority over their teenagers. That tradition started to fade in the 20th century. Still, some parents try to maintain a close watch on their children. They expect girls in particular to help out with cooking, cleaning, and other housework.

As in other countries, teenagers in South Africa don't always get along with Mom and Dad. After all, Mom and Dad may not be around very much, especially Dad. South Africa is short on jobs, which means that some parents (particularly fathers) spend a lot of time hunting for work. He may also end up using alcohol or drugs to escape the frustration of being jobless. When a father finds a job, his workplace may be far from home.

In addition, South Africa has one of the world's highest divorce rates. Nearly half of all South African marriages end in divorce. Three of every five couples who split up have children under age 18, and the mother usually gets custody of the kids.

While fathers are more likely to be absent than mothers, even Mom may not be around for her kids' teen years. AIDS and related illnesses have killed so many adults that one of every four South African teenagers has only one parent, or none at all. Many of the teens live with other relatives and treat them as parents.

Still, 90 percent of South African kids see their parents as good role models and hope to turn out like them. That's the finding of the 2005 National Youth and Victimization Study, a survey of children and teenagers by South Africa's Center for Justice and Crime Prevention. When fathers are gone, South African kids find other men to admire, such as uncles, grandfathers, or older brothers. A South African teenager may sometimes resent or ignore his parents, but deep down he generally wants to love and admire them.

In some cases, South African teens have no one to live with and must become the adult of the family and raise their younger siblings.

Outside the Family

Everyone needs friends, and South African teenagers depend on theirs for support and fun. Racial differences still divide many South Africans, but

teenagers in racially mixed cities such as Cape Town get to know teens of different colors. South African teenagers hang out with friends the way that teens in other countries do: They watch videos, play games or sports, and talk about dating.

They also keep in close touch with each other. Cell phones are especially popular. About four of every

Though teens are friendly with other ethnic groups, their closest friends are often the same ethnicity.

five South Africans have a cell phone, roughly the same number as in Japan or the United States.

South African teenagers are very attached to their cell phones. "[South African] teenagers see themselves and their cell phone as one. They love their cell phones, and they cannot imagine life without it," says a survey for the educational technology company

MobilED. "They sleep with it, eat with it, live with it."

They love the Internet as well, although Internet access isn't as widespread as cell-phone ownership. About one of every nine South Africans is an Internet user—the highest rate in sub-Saharan Africa. Teenagers and other young South Africans are among the Net's biggest fans and probably use it more than older people do. They definitely use it to keep in touch with each other. They love logging onto social networking sites such as Facebook and MySpace.

Boys & Girls Together

Like teenagers anywhere, South African teens enjoy dating. They meet people at school and at parties. Finding a boyfriend or girlfriend at the warm, summery end of the year is especially common. South Africans throw parties around that time to celebrate Christmas, New Year's Eve, the end of the matric exams, and other happy events.

Dating in South Africa, like dating in other countries, has its share of heartbreak and joy. Girls complain that boys pressure them for sex. Sometimes the pressure gets violent. Nearly all sexually active teenage girls in a 2004 survey said that they had engaged in sex at least once because someone had used physical force on them.

As in countries throughout the world, celebrations in South Africa range from huge national events to personal occasions such as graduation.

4

Something to Celebrate

DO SOUTH AFRICANS HAVE TOO MANY HOLIDAYS?

They do, according to 40 percent of the people in an informal poll by Cape Town radio stations.

Quite a few nations have about as many holidays as South Africans do (12), or even more. Tanzania, nearly 800 miles (1,300 km) north-east of South Africa, has more than 16. But every year, as the end of March approaches, South African business owners wince. In the 30 or so working days from March 21 through May 1, national holidays give employees at least six days off.

No matter how loudly the businesspeople complain, though, few South African politicians would dare to eliminate any of the country's holidays. South Africans love a good party. From the annual Dance Umbrella (a celebration of contemporary dance and movement) to the Hermanus Whale Festival to the multiday rock concert Woodstock, the country has plenty of opportunities to grab some fun.

January to December

Here is a list of South Africa's most important and popular holidays:

January 1	New Year's Day
March 21	Human Rights Day
Late March or early April	Good Friday and Easter Sunday
Monday after Easter Sunday	Family Day
April 27	Freedom Day
May 1	Workers' Day
June 16	Youth Day
August 9	Women's Day
September 24	Heritage Day
December 16	Day of Reconciliation
December 25	Christmas
December 26	Day of Goodwill

If a holiday falls on a Sunday, South Africans celebrate the holiday on the following Monday in order to give themselves a day off from work.

Days of Protest

Several of South Africa's holidays recall the time of apartheid. The Day of Reconciliation goes all the way back to December 16, 1838, when a group of Afrikaners fought an army of Zulus. Before the battle, the Afrikaners vowed to God that they would build a church if they were granted victory. After they won, Afrikaners celebrated December 16 as the Day of the Vow. In 1961, an anti-apartheid political party named the African National Congress chose December 16 to launch a campaign of sabotage and violence. After apartheid fell in 1994, the new government renamed December 16 the Day of Reconciliation and dedicated it to bringing South Africans together in peace.

Under apartheid, nonwhites had to carry a "pass book"—documents defining and restricting their right to enter areas where white people lived and worked. Nonwhites who didn't have a pass book risked arrest and punishment. The pass laws applied only to

men until 1956, when Prime Minister J.G. Strijdom considered imposing them on women. On August 9, thousands of South African women marched on the nation's capital to present petitions signed by thousands more, all asking the prime minister not to make women carry the humiliating pass books. Strijdom refused to meet with them, but their protest showed the world how firmly South Africa's black women had united against apartheid. Today South Africans celebrate August 9 as Women's Day with parties, dances, and public-spirited speeches.

On March 21, 1960, anti-apartheid activists were protesting the

Archbishop Desmond Tutu, who won the Nobel Peace Prize for his work against apartheid, danced to music at the 2005 Day of Reconciliation celebration in Cape Town.

53

Youth Day celebrations often include reenactments of the tragic events in 1976.

pass-book laws at a police station in the Sharpeville township near Johannesburg. The police opened fire, killed 69 people, and wounded nearly three times that many. The attack made the world see how brutally apartheid treated anyone who wasn't white. Now South Africans recognize March 21 as Human Rights Day. It is a time to gather for parties, political protests, or both.

Teenagers come into their own on Youth Day. By the 1970s, black South Africans were fed up with education under apartheid. The government was already teaching black students in English. In 1976, it ordered them to take courses taught in Afrikaans as well. The demand to take on a second

Religions in South Africa

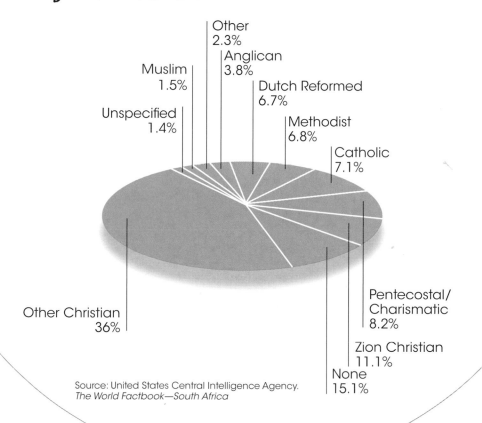

Other
2.3%

Anglican
3.8%

Muslim
1.5%

Dutch Reformed
6.7%

Unspecified
1.4%

Methodist
6.8%

Catholic
7.1%

Other Christian
36%

Pentecostal/
Charismatic
8.2%

Zion Christian
11.1%

None
15.1%

Source: United States Central Intelligence Agency.
The World Factbook—South Africa

"white" language was the last straw for the frustrated black teenagers. On June 16, thousands of them staged a protest march in Soweto. Once again, policemen killed protesters. Black South Africans all over the country rioted. Today the country throws youth concerts and other events on June 16 to honor the young rebels.

Freedom Day comes on April 27. It celebrates the date in 1994 when South Africans held their first free, post-apartheid national elections. To honor this day, politicians make speeches, musicians throw concerts, and crowds gather all over the country to celebrate.

Days of Faith

About two-thirds of all South Africans are Christians. The biggest Christian holidays have become national celebrations.

Easter falls during the autumn in South Africa. The holiday officially begins on Good Friday, continues through Easter Sunday, and concludes on Family Day. This day, the Monday after Easter, is intended as a day for families to spend together. As in other countries, observant Christians go to church on this weekend. Nearly everyone goes to picnics, parties, family gatherings, or other celebrations. Since the span from Good Friday through Family Day provides a four-day weekend, many South Africans use it for short vacations.

Christmas and the day afterward, known as the Day of Goodwill or Boxing Day, are a time for traditions such as gift giving, caroling, and family meals. South Africa's December 25 comes in midsummer, and many South Africans head outdoors to enjoy swimming, sunbathing, and other hot-weather fun.

Other Big Days

New Year's Eve and New Year's Day are as much fun in South Africa as they are in Europe or the Americas. Cape Town has a reputation for the biggest

Christmas traditions include visits from Santa Claus, also known as Sinterklaas and Father Christmas.

Up to 13,000 people dress in costume and carry umbrellas or play instruments for the Cape Town Minstrel Carnival.

celebrations, including one that dates back to the days when the city's white people kept black Africans as slaves. The whites gave the blacks only one day off—generally the second of January. The slaves seized the day with wild parties. They were known for musical performances called minstrel shows, and today Cape Town hosts a parade and multiday carnival called the Cape Town Minstrel Festival.

May 1 is Workers' Day, which celebrates the efforts of anyone who holds down a job. Labor unions and other groups use the day for rallies and protest marches. Since Workers' Day falls only four days after Freedom Day, some South Africans use both holidays and the two days between them for vacations and other escapes.

Heritage Day, on September 24, is a spring holiday. President Nelson Mandela proposed it in the 1990s to bring his often squabbling people together in celebrating the country's traditions. Since the holiday doesn't reach back to a single event, as Youth Day or Women's Day do, many South Africans simply take it as a time for a big braai.

Welcome to the Family

South African families have special days of their own. Birthdays, graduations, weddings, and other events call for congratulations, gifts, and big meals.

By law, South African teenagers become adults at age 18, but some traditional societies have their own ways of initiating kids into adulthood. Among the Xhosa people of the rural Eastern Cape, teenage boys become men by going into the wilderness, or the bush,

as South Africans call it. Over a period that can last for weeks, Xhosa men teach the boys about wilderness survival and tribal traditions.

The traditions include covering the boys in white clay and circumcising them. Unfortunately, the wilderness is not germ-free, and the boys sometimes get infected. Hundreds of boys have been hospitalized for infections that they suffered during this traditional Xhosa rite of manhood. A number of

Xhosa initiation traditions include covering the body with white clay and singing traditional songs.

laws regulate circumcision. The Eastern Cape, for instance, insists that a qualified surgeon perform the operation in a clean setting, but some people ignore the laws.

Another ritual is marriage. South Africa has one of the world's highest marriage rates. Some sources say that every year, more than 11 percent of all South Africans walk down the aisle. In other words, teenage South Africans probably go to more weddings than teenagers in Ireland, Sweden, France, and other countries with low marriage rates.

South Africans don't rush into marriage, though. Less than 5 percent get married before age 20, and the average age of marriage is 25. That's a fairly typical number for men but not for women. In neighboring Zimbabwe and Mozambique, for instance, more than 20 percent of women get married while still in their teens.

Tradition-minded black South Africans practice customs such as *lobola*. Roughly translated, lobola means "bride price." It's a payment that the groom gives to the family of the bride for the right to marry her. Originally paid in cattle, modern lobola generally is a cash payment of more than 10,000 rand (U.S.$1,238).

lobola
loh-BOH-luh

The Last Ceremony

The last ceremony for a South African comes after his or her death. Funerals in South Africa vary according to religious and ethnic traditions. Often they're public events where the dead person's family allows (or invites) the entire community to say goodbye.

Because of AIDS, many of the dead are teenagers. On average, 200 of any 100,000 South Africans ages 15 through 19 die every year—a very high rate for a country that's not at war. In Norway, by contrast, the number is only about 40 per 100,000.

A teenager lights his father's fields on fire after wheat harvest to prepare to plant corn. Nine percent of working South Africans make their living in agriculture.

5

All in a Day's Work

HALF OF ALL SOUTH AFRICAN HIGH SCHOOL STUDENTS DROP OUT TO ENTER THE JOB MARKET.
South Africa offers the strongest environment for business on the continent, and South African companies desperately need new employees. So teens should be able to find work easily. Unfortunately, employers often hire workers from other countries, while South Africans remain jobless for months at a stretch.

Young South Africans are among the most likely to go jobless. Half of all South Africans who want jobs, ages 15 to 24, are unemployed.

They add up to one-third of the entire jobless population.

A large part of the problem is a national skills shortage. South African employers need workers trained in high finance, information technology, engineering, and other intensely technical fields. But fewer than half of all South African teenagers go to college, and 85 percent of college students drop out before they can graduate.

Even the ones who do get degrees aren't always qualified for the jobs available. About 40 percent of South Africa's recent college graduates majored in education, the

Division of Labor in South Africa

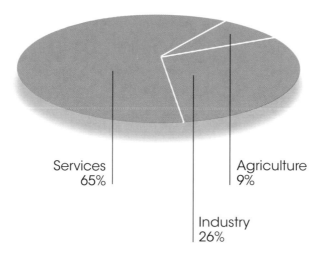

Services
65%

Agriculture
9%

Industry
26%

Source: United States Central Intelligence Agency.
The World Factbook—South Africa

arts, or the human-
ities (literature, history,
and related fields). Only about 20
percent specialized in business, engineering, or other fields with employers
that are hiring. As a result, employers
desperately need to hire people. South
Africans desperately want to be hired,
but they just don't have the skills.

It's not all bleak, though. The country has nearly 13 million working people.
The largest groups of South African workers are manual laborers, salespeople,
craftspeople, and ser-
vice providers ranging from
nurses to real estate agents. South Africa
is a rainbow nation not just in race, but
in the variety of its jobs.

Animals, Plants & People
About a million South Africans work
in farming, fishing, or forestry. Sales
of plant and animal products generate
nearly 90 billion South African rand
(U.S.$11.1 billion) per year. It totals
about 15 percent of the country's wealth.

The most important farm products are animals. The biggest moneymakers are cattle and poultry, which account for about one-third of all farm income. In addition, South African ranches raise sheep, pigs, and other animals.

Only 12 percent of South Africa's land is suitable for raising crops, but farmers use it thoroughly. The most lucrative plant product is corn, grown mostly in the provinces North-West, the Free State, Mpumalanga, and KwaZulu-Natal. Other big crops are fruit, particularly apples (primarily in the Western Cape); pineapples (largely in the Eastern Cape); grapes; and pears. Other farms grow grains such as wheat and barley; vegetables including potatoes, tomatoes, onions, and cabbages; and other crops such as sugarcane.

South Africans run a number of family farms, but giant corporations own most of the land and hire most of the farmworkers. However, in recent years, they've been hiring fewer and fewer, so the number of farmworkers is shrinking.

Big companies also control much of South Africa's business in wood and products made of wood, such as furniture. Forest plantations cover about 5,800 square miles (15,800 sq km), mostly in Mpumalanga and KwaZulu-Natal provinces.

The country's first vineyards were planted near Cape Town. Wine exports are a growing industry.

Meanwhile, the fishing industry, based mostly in and near the Western Cape, brings in about 1 billion rand (U.S.$130 million) every year. Half of the money is from a codlike fish called hake and the other half from squid, lobster, and other seafood.

The Underground

Crops aren't the only riches in South Africa's soil. Under the ground is a fortune in minerals. The mining industry has been declining slowly over the past several years, but it's still a powerhouse. South Africa is the world's largest producer of gold. It's also one of the top sources of iron, platinum (used in jewelry and electrical components), manganese (for making steel), chromium (everything from dyes to diet pills), and other metals. In addition, the South African company De Beers controls half or more of the world's diamond supply. Overall, mining contributes more than 100 billion rand (U.S.$13.2 billion) to the South African economy every year.

Gold miners drill holes into rock, then fill them with dynamite. The blast removes the gold.

Land Use

- Cereal crops
- Forest
- Manufacturing
- Nomadic livestock
- Pasture livestock
- Plantation crops

South Africa
Land use map

ZIMBABWE

Bananas

LIMPOPO

MOZAMBIQUE

Polokwane

BOTSWANA

Tobacco

Nelspruit

Pretoria

MPUMALANGA

Mafikeng

Johannesburg

Sandton

NORTH-WEST

GAUTENG

Corn

Sugarcane

SWAZILAND

Gold

Potatoes

Gold

Cattle

Diamonds

Sugarcane

KWAZULU-NATAL

Kimberley

FREE STATE

Wheat

NAMIBIA

Diamonds

Bloemfontein

Diamonds

LESOTHO

Pietermaritzburg

Diamonds

Durban

NORTHERN CAPE

Sugarcane

Poultry

EASTERN CAPE

Sheep

Bhisho

Tea

Barley

N

W   E

S

WESTERN CAPE

Knysna

Citrus

Cape
Town

Wheat

Port
Elizabeth

0   50   100 mi.

0   50   100 km

South Africa's mining companies employ more than 450,000 people, most of them in northern provinces such as North-West, Gauteng, Mpumalanga, and Limpopo. The North-West province alone has well over 150,000 mining-industry workers, more than any other province.

Mining is dangerous, though. Explosions and falling rocks kill about 200 miners every year and injure thousands more.

Making & Building

After farmers harvest crops and ranchers raise livestock and miners dig out metals, other people turn them into finished products. More than a million South Africans make everything from clothes to high-tech electronics.

The farmers' immense harvests feed the manufacturing business that hires the most people: food processing. Every year, processing and packaging workers produce thousands of tons of flour, refined sugar, cooking oils, pet and cattle food, baked goods, and beverages ranging from wine to fruit juices and soft drinks. Canned foods, including fruits, vegetables, and fish, are big business, too.

In addition to food, the fields of farms and ranches supply the raw materials for fabric manufacturing. Nearly 200,000 people turn cotton, wool, and leather into textiles, clothing, and footwear. However, Chinese companies make and sell similar products for less money. This competition hurts South African businesses and threatens South African jobs. As a result, South Africa's government charges Chinese companies high import fees for selling their clothes in the country.

Metalwork is another huge area of manufacturing; it employs nearly 300,000 people. South Africa produces about 11 million tons (10 million metric

A Hard Day's Work

South Africans who have jobs work hard at them. A typical workday starts between 7 and 8 A.M. and usually runs until about 5 P.M., although many South Africans work overtime.

Once diamonds are mined, they have to be sorted and polished before they are sold to the consumer.

tons) of steel every year and has become the African continent's biggest steel-maker. South Africans are also strong in refining and molding most of the other metals that the country's miners dig out of the ground.

Much of the metal is turned into machines. The auto industry is one of the biggest areas of South African manufacturing. Gauteng province alone has factories assembling cars for General Motors, Toyota, Volkswagen, BMW, Ford, and other automakers. South Africans also produce high-tech electronics, from radios and televisions to precise scientific equipment.

Other South Africans are busy making chemicals. The chemical industry accounts for about 25 percent of all South African manufacturing. Liquid fuels such as petroleum are about one-third of the chemical business, plastics take up one-fifth, and smaller sectors ranging from rubber to drugs contribute as well.

At Your Service

Millions of South Africans don't make, build, or raise anything, but they offer services to improve lives. Among them are doctors, hairdressers, travel agents, janitors, waiters, and security guards. Some experts say that the world of services offers more jobs than any other South African industry, and it's the fastest-growing part of South Africa's economy.

Bankers, stockbrokers, accountants, and insurance agents fill one of the service sector's biggest areas: banking

As the black middle-income level slowly grows, more service-oriented businesses crop up.

With the numbers of black workers in banking and finance jobs increasing, the financial status of blacks slowly improves.

and finance. This world of investment and money-lending also generates jobs for support employees such as clerks and secretaries. The center of their activity is Johannesburg, the financial capital of the African continent. This city is home to FirstRand and the Standard Bank Group, Africa's biggest banks.

Some experts count salespeople as service providers, while others put them in another category: trade. From roadside fruit vendors to executives who export shiploads of Toyotas, buying and selling gives jobs to nearly 3 million South Africans. Retail stores in particular hire large numbers of workers, including teenagers. South Africans don't shop from home on the Internet as much as North Americans or Europeans do. As a result, department stores and shopping malls can get full of customers. Smaller shops have a harder time, particularly in townships and rural areas where people have little or no money.

Nothing to Do

South Africa's industries provide a lot of jobs but not enough to employ everyone who wants work. About 25 percent of all job seekers can't find a job. Millions

Unemployed people gather daily in hope of finding temporary work.

of other South Africans have simply quit looking for jobs. Together, the two groups raise unemployment close to 40 percent, one of the highest jobless rates in the world.

The problem hits black South Africans the hardest. Their rate of unemployment is six times that of whites. Most blacks who do have jobs occupy the lower rungs of the business ladder. Even though they're a huge majority of the nation's people, black South Africans are only a tiny minority of the country's corporate presidents and other executives.

To raise the number of black South Africans in the job market, the national government has set up Black Economic Empowerment (BEE). It's a program that helps black South Africans start their own businesses and pushes companies to hire and promote black people. BEE's progress has been slow, though. What's more, some white South Africans resent its existence. They believe that companies reject qualified white job applicants and instead hire incompetent black workers just because of their skin color.

Tomorrow's Work

South Africa's teenagers know that they face a tough job market. In a poll of students that asked what they'd do if they became president, the top answer was "create more jobs."

But if you ask South African high school students what they want to be when they grow up, they give a variety of answers: lawyer, businessman or businesswoman, accountant, actor, teacher, writer, doctor, and so on. Even though their country is having trouble supplying work for everyone, South African teens aren't about to give up.

Formal vs. Informal

South Africa has two kinds of businesses. Formal businesses register with the government, operate according to laws and regulations, and employ about three-quarters of all working South Africans. The informal sector includes sidewalk vendors, small shopkeepers, and other people who don't bother much with government paperwork. Generally, people in the informal sector earn much less than people on the formal side.

71

Cape Town residents celebrated after the 2004 announcement that South Africa would host the 2010 World Cup.

6

Celebrating Soccer & Other Pastimes

EVERY FOUR YEARS, MORE THAN A BILLION PEOPLE GO CRAZY OVER A CUP. To determine the world's best soccer team, the Fédération Internationale de Football Association (FIFA) holds a monthlong series of nation-against-nation playoffs. The winner gets FIFA's World Cup trophy. People in more than 200 countries follow the playoffs on television, while millions of fans, journalists, and others flood the cities that host the event.

In 2004, when FIFA picked South Africa to host the 2010 World Cup, people from Cape Town to Limpopo erupted in some of the biggest explosions of national joy since the end of apartheid. Post-apartheid South Africa was only 10 years old. Yet FIFA had declared that the country—the first African nation to host the games—was the equal of previous hosts such as France, Italy, and the United States.

Some of the happiest South Africans were teenagers. Young South Africans see a lot of unemployment, poverty, crime, AIDS, and other troubles. They love to escape it—whether the escape takes the form of a TV show, a concert, or the world's biggest soccer championship.

The Big Beat

South African teenagers love music. Rock, hip-hop, ballads, gospel, and rhythm and blues (R&B) are among their favorite styles. Some of the record industry's biggest stars perform at places such as Pretoria's 45,000-seat Loftus Stadium.

Ask a South African teenager to name his favorite band or performer, and you'll get answers that include stars from the United States and the United Kingdom. South African teens adore the sleek, warm, and danceable tunes from the Barbados-born American star Rihanna, the British trio Sugababes' steely soul, English singer Mika's cheerful funk, and American Chris Brown's pop-flavored R&B. They also love the crowd-pleasing sounds of other stars ranging from Britney Spears to Kanye West.

South African musicians aren't quite as popular as the British and American idols, but some have developed fans among South African teens. Danny K, for instance, sings smooth soul with a hard beat. The Dirty Skirts, a quartet of new-wave indie rockers,

Danny K has served as an ambassador for Nelson Mandela's campaign against HIV/AIDS.

mixes catchy rhythms with desperate-sounding vocals. The hard-rock trio Seether explores the gloomy edge of heavy metal with songs such as "Don't Believe" and "Like Suicide."

kwaito
KWY-toh

Metal, rock, and soul originally came from Britain and the United States, but South Africa has sounds of its own. *Kwaito* is a form of dance music that rose out of the townships. Kwaito performers don't play instruments; instead, like hip-hop stars, they perform to prerecorded beats. And like hip-hop, kwaito is not just music but an entire culture with its own tough, cocky attitude, slang, and clothing.

Watching the Tube

South Africa has a thriving television industry. Several national networks and hundreds of local stations broadcast programs in the 11 official languages. The most popular shows are soap operas and other dramas. The biggest of them all is *Generations*, a soap opera that went on the air not long after apartheid ended in 1994. *Generations* shows upper-class and middle-class black South Africans getting themselves into the same romantic scandals as characters in *The Bold and the Beautiful* (a mostly white American soap opera that's also a hit in South Africa). Nearly as popular as *Generations* is *Zone 14*, which centers on conflicts among township families who own a soccer team. Huge audiences also follow *Usindiso*, a new Christian-oriented religious drama.

South Africans watch other types of shows, too. The reality series *Zola 7* follows its host as he talks authority figures into solving a family's crises or getting the right job for a talented but poor young man. *Yizo Yizo*, a gritty drama, puts its young characters through rough situations involving AIDS, physical abuse, and even murder. For laughs, teenagers watch *Everybody Hates Chris* and other American comedies starring black actors. They make sure to turn on soccer matches and other sporting events. They also tune in

The Digital Screen

South African teenagers who can afford a PlayStation or other electronic equipment spend hours playing video and computer games. Games are popular Christmas gifts, and one of the country's most heavily trafficked Internet destinations is the gaming Web site GameSpot.

Charlize Theron was given a symbolic gift of a gold ore lump by South African President Thabo Mbeki following her Oscar win.

to movies, especially action adventures such as *The Fast and the Furious* and *The Mask of Zorro.*

At the Movies

South Africans see American movies in the theaters as well as on TV. South Africa's film industry tries hard to compete, but it's simply too small to pull audiences away from the glamour of American stars such as George Clooney or Eddie Murphy.

Still, South Africans have turned a few of their own into stars. Leon Schuster, for instance, makes broad comedies such as *Mama Jack,* in which Schuster's character escapes from the police by posing as a woman. When the movie came to South Africa's theaters in 2005, it quickly became a huge national hit.

Another South African has become a major international star. Charlize Theron was born on August 7, 1975, in northwest Gauteng's farm country. As a teenager, she left South Africa for Europe and became a prominent fashion model. By age 19, she was living in Hollywood and starting to act in movies. Her career moved fast. In 2004, she won an Academy Award as best actress for playing a murderer in the true-crime movie *Monster.*

The Sporting Life

South Africans are wild for sports, even though millions of young South African kids and teenagers haven't had much chance to play. Most townships don't

South Africans of all ages enjoy playing soccer.

have many parks or playgrounds. What's more, most schools in townships and rural areas usually don't have enough money to build and maintain gyms, playing fields, or swimming pools. Still, teenagers practically worship top teams and players. Their favorite sports are soccer (also known as football) and two British games, rugby and cricket.

Rugby involves two teams running with a ball or kicking it to get the ball past a goal line. It has traditionally been a middle-class or upper-class sport. In South Africa, rugby is a favorite among

77

whites and, to a lesser extent, colored South Africans. Most of the nation's top players are white, including the majority of the national rugby team, the Springboks. Some black South Africans have complained that a nation so heavily black should not send a mostly white squad to represent the country at international tournaments.

Cricket is a little more popular than rugby. Cricket players swing a flat, wooden paddle (called a bat) to hit a

South Africa won the 2007 Rugby World Cup.

Ashwell Prince was 29 years old when he became the first nonwhite captain of South Africa's cricket team.

hard ball through the poles of a wooden fork called a wicket. The opposing team's players try to stop the ball. Like rugby, cricket in South Africa has largely been a white sport, and a quota system has forced teams to add black and colored players. But after 2006, when black player Ashwell Prince became the national team's first black captain, the quotas ended.

South Africans like other sports as well. Plenty of teenagers, for instance, play netball, a game similar to basketball. But the biggest sport of all is soccer. If anything unites all South Africans—urban, rural, poor, rich, black, white, and all else—soccer is it. If a school or neighborhood has any kind of athletic area, it's likely to be a soccer field. Millions of South African teenagers follow the local and national teams, and the top players become national heroes.

Getting Out

Like teenagers almost anywhere, South African teens like to go out of town on vacation. Many of them are too poor to take a lot of trips, though.

Young South Africans who can afford to leave town on vacation often do it in December. The weather is hot, and the Christmas season and the end of the school year provide days off. Many high school and college students head to the beaches of Cape Town, Durban, and other areas along the southern coast.

In holiday-heavy April and at other times of the year, thousands of South Africans leave for resorts like Kruger National Park, a lush wildlife preserve on the eastern edge of Limpopo and Mpumalanga. Inside the park's more than 4.9 million acres (2 million hectares)—an area bigger than all of Hawaii, Swaziland, or Lebanon—South Africans go hiking, camping, and sightseeing, or even go on a safari.

South Africans who go beyond their home country often don't go far. Usually they travel to nearby nations. Many head into Mozambique, just over the border from Kruger National Park. Namibia, Lesotho, and Swaziland are popular destinations as well.

Elephants drink from a water hole at Kruger National Park, which was named after Afrikaner political leader Paul Kruger.

South Africa
Topographical
map

ZIMBABWE

Limpopo River

LIMPOPO

Kruger
National
Park

MOZAMBIQUE

Polokwane

BOTSWANA

Kalahari
Gemsbok
National Park

Mafikeng

Pretoria

Nelspruit

MPUMALANGA

Johannesburg

Sandton

GAUTENG

NORTH-WEST

SWAZILAND

Kalahari
Desert

Vaal River

FREE STATE

KWAZULU-
NATAL

NAMIBIA

Orange River

Kimberley

Mount
Njesuthi

Bloemfontein

Orange River

LESOTHO

Pietermaritzburg

Durban

NORTHERN CAPE

EASTERN CAPE

Great
Karoo

Bhisho

N

WESTERN CAPE

Little
Karoo

W   E

S

0   50   100 mi.

Robben
Island

Table
Mountain

0   50   100 km

Cape
Town

Knysna

Port
Elizabeth

Looking Ahead

IN 2006, THE SOUTH AFRICAN RESEARCH COMPANY FUTUREFACT POLLED THE NATION'S TEENAGERS. The company found that 83 percent felt more confident than they had a year earlier. About 89 percent said that they wanted to help improve their country, and 94 percent believed that South Africa could become a truly wealthy and powerful nation.

South Africa's teenagers may suffer from enormous problems, but they're not giving up. The first South Africans to grow up after apartheid believe that they and their country are getting better all the time. If they're right, their country—already the richest, most advanced nation in sub-Saharan Africa—has an amazing future ahead.

At a Glance

Official name: Republic of South Africa

Capital: Cape Town (legislative), Pretoria (administrative), Bloemfontein (judicial)

People

Population: 43,997,828

Population by age group:
0–14 years: 29.1%
15–64 years: 65.5%
65 years and over: 5.4%

Life expectancy at birth: 42.5 years

Official languages:
Afrikaans, English, Ndebele, Pedi, Sotho, Tsonga, Tswana, Swati, Venda, Xhosa, Zulu

Religions:

Zion Christian 11.1%
Pentecostal/Charismatic 8.2%
Catholic 7.1%
Methodist 6.8%
Dutch Reformed 6.7%
Anglican 3.8%

Muslim 1.5%
Other 2.3%
Other Christian 36%
Unspecified 1.4%
None 15.1%

Legal ages
Alcohol consumption: 18
Driver's license: 18
Employment: 15
Marriage: 18 (16 with parental approval)
Military service: 18
School: required through age 15
Voting: 18

Government

Type of government: Constitutional democracy

Chief of state: President, elected by the National Assembly for a five-year term

Head of government: President

Lawmaking body: Parliament, divided into two houses, the National Assembly and the Council of Provinces, elected by popular vote

Administrative divisions: Nine provinces

Independence: April 27, 1994, the day of the first free, all-races national election, celebrated annually as Freedom Day

National symbols:
National animal: Springbok
National bird: Blue crane
National fish: Galjoen
National flower: King protea
National tree: Real yellowwood

Geography

Total Area: 487,965 square miles (1,219,912 square kilometers)

Climate: Generally warm, with dry weather on the western side and tropical weather in the east

Highest point: Mount Njesuthi, 11,246 feet (3,408 meters)

Lowest point: Atlantic Ocean, sea level

Major rivers: Limpopo, Orange, Vaal

Major landforms: Kalahari Desert, Drakensberg Mountains, Great Karoo, Table Mountain

Economy

Currency: Rand

Population below poverty line: 50%

Major natural resources: Gold, chromium, antimony, coal, iron ore, manganese, nickel, phosphates, tin, uranium, gem diamonds, platinum, copper, vanadium, salt, natural gas

Major agricultural products: Poultry, cattle, citrus and other fruit, milk, corn, potatoes, other vegetables

Major exports: Gold and other metals, metal products, precious stones and other minerals, food

Major imports: Petroleum, machinery, chemicals, textiles

Historical Timeline

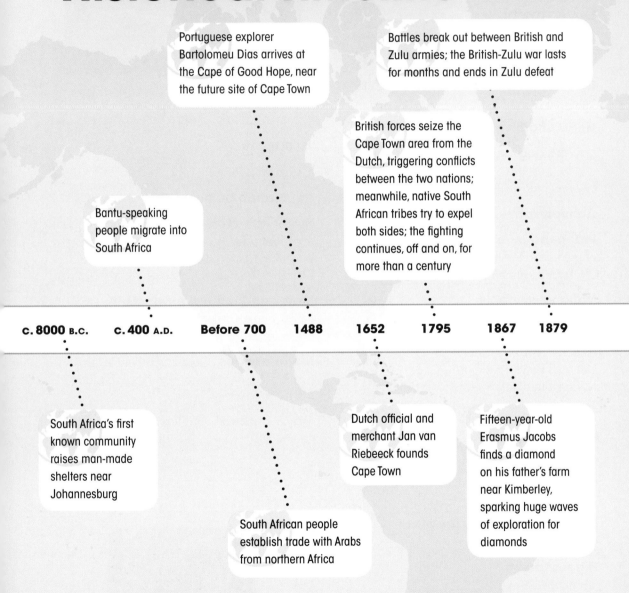

Portuguese explorer Bartolomeu Dias arrives at the Cape of Good Hope, near the future site of Cape Town

Battles break out between British and Zulu armies; the British-Zulu war lasts for months and ends in Zulu defeat

British forces seize the Cape Town area from the Dutch, triggering conflicts between the two nations; meanwhile, native South African tribes try to expel both sides; the fighting continues, off and on, for more than a century

Bantu-speaking people migrate into South Africa

| c. 8000 B.C. | c. 400 A.D. | Before 700 | 1488 | 1652 | 1795 | 1867 | 1879 |

South Africa's first known community raises man-made shelters near Johannesburg

Dutch official and merchant Jan van Riebeeck founds Cape Town

Fifteen-year-old Erasmus Jacobs finds a diamond on his father's farm near Kimberley, sparking huge waves of exploration for diamonds

South African people establish trade with Arabs from northern Africa

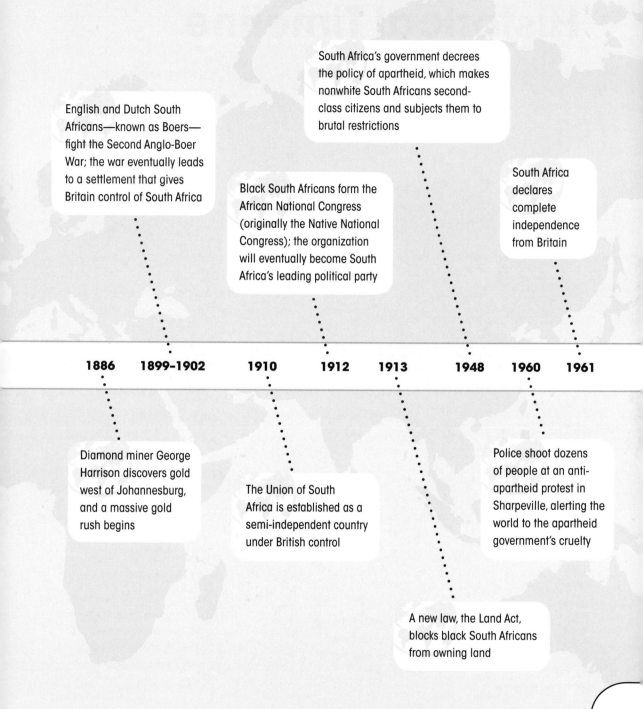

English and Dutch South Africans—known as Boers—fight the Second Anglo-Boer War; the war eventually leads to a settlement that gives Britain control of South Africa

South Africa's government decrees the policy of apartheid, which makes nonwhite South Africans second-class citizens and subjects them to brutal restrictions

Black South Africans form the African National Congress (originally the Native National Congress); the organization will eventually become South Africa's leading political party

South Africa declares complete independence from Britain

1886   **1899–1902**   **1910**   **1912**   **1913**   **1948**   **1960**   **1961**

Diamond miner George Harrison discovers gold west of Johannesburg, and a massive gold rush begins

The Union of South Africa is established as a semi-independent country under British control

Police shoot dozens of people at an anti-apartheid protest in Sharpeville, alerting the world to the apartheid government's cruelty

A new law, the Land Act, blocks black South Africans from owning land

Historical Timeline

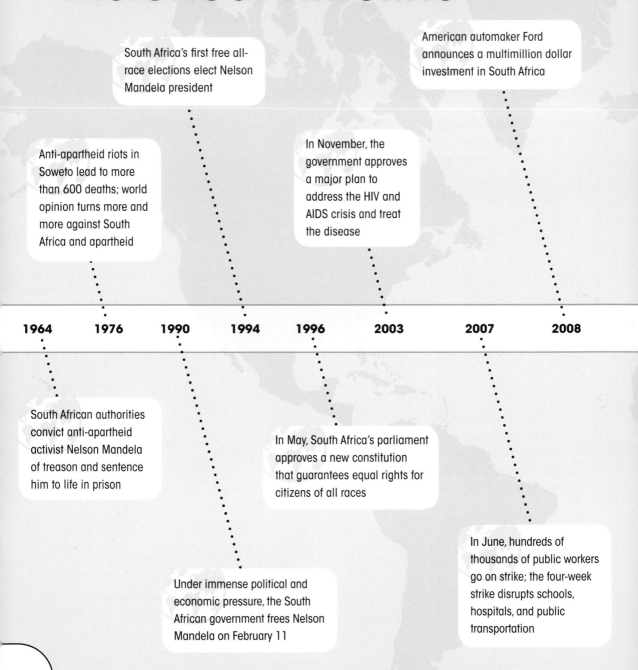

South Africa's first free all-race elections elect Nelson Mandela president

American automaker Ford announces a multimillion dollar investment in South Africa

Anti-apartheid riots in Soweto lead to more than 600 deaths; world opinion turns more and more against South Africa and apartheid

In November, the government approves a major plan to address the HIV and AIDS crisis and treat the disease

1964 **1976** **1990** **1994** **1996** **2003** **2007** **2008**

South African authorities convict anti-apartheid activist Nelson Mandela of treason and sentence him to life in prison

In May, South Africa's parliament approves a new constitution that guarantees equal rights for citizens of all races

Under immense political and economic pressure, the South African government frees Nelson Mandela on February 11

In June, hundreds of thousands of public workers go on strike; the four-week strike disrupts schools, hospitals, and public transportation

Glossary

Afrikaans | language of South Africans descended from Dutch settlers

Afrikaner | South African descended from Dutch settlers

AIDS | abbreviation for acquired immune deficiency syndrome, a disease of the immune system that makes people more likely to catch infections and get some rare cancers that are often fatal; usually transmitted by sexual activity or contaminated blood

apartheid | former government policy of racial segregation and discrimination against nonwhites

braai | barbecue; a favorite South African way of cooking

circumcision | surgical removal of part of the reproductive organs; in males, the foreskin of the penis is removed; in females, part or all of the clitoris is removed

fertility rate | average number of children each woman has during her lifetime

HIV | abbreviation for human immunodeficiency virus, any of a group of viruses that infect and destroy helper T cells, causing a reduction in their numbers and leading to AIDS

matrics | important series of exams near the end of Grade 12 that determine whether students go to college

MXit | popular instant-messaging system for cell phones and computers

Glossary

quota system	|	policy requiring that a specified number or percentage of minority group members be accepted or hired
rand	|	currency of South Africa
sub-Saharan	|	refers to the part of Africa that lies south of the Sahara Desert
ubuntu	|	unifying spirit of community and shared humanity—a central concept for South Africa's diverse population
Xhosa	|	South African people known for its leaders in the nation's government
Zulu	|	largest group of South Africans, primarily living in the KwaZulu-Natal province

Additional Resources

IN THE LIBRARY

Fiction and nonfiction titles to further
enhance your introduction to teens in South
Africa, past and present.

Gordon, Sheila. *Waiting for the Rain: A
    Novel of South Africa*. New York:
    Orchard Books, 1987.

McKissack, Patricia. *Nzingha, Warrior
    Queen of Matamba*. New York:
    Scholastic, 2000.

Naidoo, Beverly. *No Turning Back: A
    Novel of South Africa*. New York:
    HarperCollins Publishers, 1997.

Downing, David. *Apartheid in South
    Africa*. Chicago: Heinemann, 2004.

Kramer, Ann. *Mandela: The Rebel
    Who Led His Nation to Freedom*.
    Washington, D.C.: National
    Geographic Children's Books, 2005.

Oppong, Joseph R. *Africa South of
    the Sahara*. Philadelphia: Chelsea
    House Publishers, 2005.

ON THE WEB

For more information on this topic,
use FactHound.
1. Go to www.facthound.com
2. Type in this book ID: 0756538548
3. Click on the *Fetch It* button.

Look for more Global Connections books.

Teens in Australia	*Teens in France*	*Teens in Morocco*	*Teens in Spain*
Teens in Brazil	*Teens in Ghana*	*Teens in Nepal*	*Teens in Turkey*
Teens in Canada	*Teens in India*	*Teens in Nigeria*	*Teens in the U.S.A.*
Teens in China	*Teens in Iran*	*Teens in Peru*	*Teens in Venezuela*
Teens in Cuba	*Teens in Israel*	*Teens in the Philippines*	*Teens in Vietnam*
Teens in Egypt	*Teens in Japan*	*Teens in Russia*	
Teens in England	*Teens in Kenya*	*Teens in Saudi Arabia*	
Teens in Finland	*Teens in Mexico*	*Teens in South Korea*	

Source Notes

Page 9, line 9: Nelson Mandela. "Inaugural Address." 10 May 1994. 14 April 2008. www.wsu.edu:8080/~wldciv/world_civ_reader/world_civ_reader_2/mandela.html

Page 17, column 2, line 34: Michael Muller. "'Massive Growth' in Drug Addiction Among Teenagers." *Mail & Guardian* Online. 3 February 2006. 14 April 2008. www.mg.co.za/articlePage.aspx?articleid=263275&area=/breaking_news/breaking_news__national/

Page 23, column 1, line 17: University of the Witwatersrand, Johannesburg. "South Africaness—How the New Generation of Teenagers View South Africa." 22 September 2004. 14 April 2008. web.wits.ac.za/Academic/Health/Research/BirthTo20/Research/EditorialReleases/EditorialReleases2004.htm

Page 26, column 1, line 11: Robin Mackey. "32. Sniper-man and Other 'Pneu's." Weblog entry. 15 Dec. 2005. 14 April 2008. www.sawubona.ca/RoBlog/C584549232/E20061125202729/index.html

Page 35, column 1, line 1: Omniglot Writing Systems and Languages of the World. 1 May 2008. www.omniglot.com

Page 35, column 2, line 1: "South Africa." GeoNative. 1 May 2008. www.geocities.com/Athens/9479/zulu.html

Page 39, column 2, line 5: Laura Sessions Stepp. "In South Africa, D.C. Girls Tally Lessons Learned." *Washington Post*. 10 July 2007. 14 April 2008. www.washingtonpost.com/wp-dyn/content/article/2007/07/09/AR2007070901322.html

Page 48, column 1, line 5: C. Oelofse, A. De Jager, and M. Ford. "The Digital Profile of a Teenage Cell Phone Learner." 2006. 14 April 2008. www2.uiah.fi/~tleinone/mobiled/christa_mlearn2006.pdf.

Page 71, column 1, line 35: "South Africaness—How the New Generation of Teenagers View South Africa."

Pages 84–85, At a Glance: United States. Central Intelligence Agency. *The World Factbook—South Africa*. 20 March 2008. 14 April 2008. https://www.cia.gov/library/publications/the-world-factbook/geos/sf.html

Select Bibliography

"Crime Situation in SA." South African Government Information. 2 July 2007. 1 Dec. 2007. www.info.gov.za/issues/crime/Crime%20Situation%20in%20SA_Dir%20Sally_2006%202007%20financial%20year.pdf

Falola, Toyin, ed. *Teen Life in Africa*. Westport, Conn.: Greenwood Press, 2004.

"Friendship and Challenge: Soccer in South Africa." University Credit Union, 8 Oct. 2007. http://googolplex.cuna.org/12433/cnote/story.html?doc_id=1000

Hunter-Gault, Charlayne. *New News out of Africa: Uncovering Africa's Renaissance*. New York: Oxford University Press, 2006.

Leoschut, Lezanne, and Patrick Burton. *How Rich the Rewards?: Results of the 2005 National Youth Victimisation Study*. Cape Town: Centre for Justice and Crime Prevention, 2006.

Lomas, Yvonne C. "Life As a Teen in ... South Africa." *Ambassador Youth*. August–September 2007.

Pearce, Justin. "School Day: South Africa Pupils Interact." BBC News, 14 June 2006. 9 Dec. 2007. http://news.bbc.co.uk/2/hi/africa/ 5076646.stm

Richter, Linda, et al. *The Status of Youth Report 2003: Young People in South Africa*. Midrand, South Africa: Umsobomvu Youth Fund, 2005.

Schüssler, Mike. "The 6th South African Employment Report: Skills Shortage—Urban Legend or Fact?" United Association of South Africa. 6 Dec. 2007. 13 Dec. 2007. www.uasa.co.za/reports/ EmpReportNo6.pdf

Statistics South Africa. *Labour Force Survey, March 2007*. Pretoria: Statistics South Africa, 2007.

United States. Central Intelligence Agency. *The World Factbook—South Africa*. 20 March 2008. 14 April 2008. https://www.cia. gov/library/publications/the-world-factbook/geos/sf.html

Wines, Michael. "Reaching for the Sky." *New York Times Upfront*. 5 Sept. 2005.

Index

About the Author
David Seidman

David Seidman has written more than 30 books on subjects ranging from Latino Americans to Spider-Man to the F/A-18 warplane. He has been an editor at the *Los Angeles Times* and Disney Publishing, a novelist, a stand-up comedian, a comic-book writer, and a teacher of writing at University of California, Los Angeles. He lives in West Hollywood, California.

About the Content Adviser
Rachel Bray, Ph.D.

Rachel Bray holds a Ph.D. in social anthropology from the University of Durham, England. As a research fellow at the University of Cape Town's Centre for Social Science Research, Dr. Bray studies the lives of children and adolescents in three communities in the Cape Peninsula. She has also conducted research on the effect of HIV/AIDS on South Africa's children.

border to border · teen to teen · border to border · teen to teen · border to border